Jeannie

Peace And blessing to you and yours, May God bring you must Joy, That which is within is but a token of my joy, thus I share with you
Love
M Dan

Reflections Bring About a Revelation

Author:
Marcellus Dean

Bloomington, IN  Milton Keynes, UK

AuthorHouse™
1663 Liberty Drive, Suite 200
Bloomington, IN 47403
www.authorhouse.com
Phone: 1-800-839-8640

AuthorHouse™ UK Ltd.
500 Avebury Boulevard
Central Milton Keynes, MK9 2BE
www.authorhouse.co.uk
Phone: 08001974150

© *2008 Marcellus Dean. All rights reserved.*

No part of this book may be reproduced, stored in a retrieval system, or transmitted by any means without the written permission of the author.

First published by AuthorHouse 1/18/2008

ISBN: 978-1-4343-1033-0 (sc)

Printed in the United States of America
Bloomington, Indiana

This book is printed on acid-free paper.

Preface

The poems that you are about to read tell life's stories, it's ups and downs, its trials and tribulations and most of all its hopes and reassurances. It is through Jesus Christ that I've been blessed to become the instrument in which each poem is written with you in mind. I am blessed to be able to take what was given unto me and reach out to those searching, but have yet to find. I am lending a hand to those who feel the world has left them behind. No, I don't claim to have all the answers but throughout this book there lies many clues, and it is because of you that I wish to share these words of courage, truth and wisdom. Not according to me but according to you, for truly you've inspired me through many conversations, which touched me deeply. I've had revelations as your word's resonated throughout my endeavor. You ask yourself – "How can this be?" - when we have never met.

Everybody has a story to tell, yet are unwilling for fear of no one understanding, so if I may, let me speak for you as you find your place amongst the poems. God has given me so much and I wish to share it with you. So, as you find yourself within this book know that I owe it all to you. Through writing I've found peace and understanding of what life can ultimately be. There truly is healing in the words you are about to read -- just take your time, read, digest and you will see. This book will bring about a change in your life no matter what the situation you now face. My dream is for my poems to be the vehicle that allows you to find that peaceful place within your soul. It's not by chance that we've met and that you have this book in your hands, it's all according to God's plan.

Table of Contents

CHAPTER ONE 1
    Reassuring Despite Doubt
    "Words to Soothe the Soul"

CHAPTER TWO 15
    Redefining Self
    "Words of Growth"

CHAPTER THREE 35
    Social Awareness
    "Words of Knowledge"

CHAPTER FOUR 53
    Unbeknownst to You
    "Words of Healing"

CHAPTER FIVE 73
    She Speaks
    "Words From Her Heart"

CHAPTER SIX 89
    Unspoken Words
    "Words That Go Unsaid"

CHAPTER SEVEN 103
    With You in Mind
    "Words to soothe a troubled spirit"

CHAPTER EIGHT 115
    Within His Voice
    "Words to Strengthen the Male Soul"

AUTHOR'S BIOGRAPHY 133

Chapter One

REASSURING DESPITE DOUBT

"Words to Soothe the Soul"

A Poem 4 U

To the lady who has her whole life in front of her, this poem is 4 u and for those moments when you sit in despair.
Contemplating your life as often as you do, this poem was written to help you get through.
I know life's not easy as you begin to find yourself, just trust in Christ and you find strength when you have nothing left.

A poem 4 u is what God placed on my heart, so I wrote a few words as you embark upon a new start.
Wherever the road takes you, you need not fret, because as long as you believe in you, you'll have no regrets.
To those who don't understand your transformation, let not your heart be troubled they only seek justification.

With the way the world is today it truly is nice to know, there is someone out there who knows what it means to grow.
Thus a poem 4 u was instilled in my heart, to shed some light on your world when things seem dark.
Always remember that God has not brought you this far in life, for you to fall by the way because of your decision wrong or right.

What will be the outcome that's not for you to decide, just step out on faith and enjoy the ride?
Take life as it comes and if it was meant to be, then surely you will be blessed with the ability to see.
Never let the thought of you being alone be your biggest fear, because the purpose of this poem is to let you know Jesus Christ is always near.

You see the truest passion of our existence comes from helping another, and thus this poem 4 u comes from a real true brother.

Another Man's Treasure

As you lock your self away from the world to gather your thoughts, please realize you've given him more power than you ought.
Surely you had a life before you two met, so why live this time wondering with tears of regret.
It's not yours to claim and you need not feel a shame, because the loss of one man truly is a better man's gain.

What life may dictate comes with a price one must pay to create, a better understanding of ones self in finding their soul mate.
Nothing is left to chance once you've been down that road; just remember there is one who is willing to help you carry that load.
If you were told that you were still a treasure, would you believe it or would you feel that you didn't measure.

Because despite your displeasure of what has transpired, there truly is another one waiting for you to come alive.
So many see that very thing that you are unwilling to see, the true value of a woman who needs to put her mind at ease.
Yes it's hard to move on because your feelings are so strong, but you must realize your worth and not let it linger so long.

You are a precious jewel a rare commodity in deed, you are that blessed treasure that one seeks and he will unconditionally, fulfill all your needs.
To be cherished by one and admired by all men, so take this moment to reflect and rise up from whence you've fallen.
God does not make mistakes you had to learn what it would take, and now that you've paid the price, step out on faith and embrace your mate.

What was must give way to only that which you can measure, not of the past but today and tomorrow for you truly are another man's treasure.

Be Not Afraid

Be not afraid of the unknown and worry not of what tomorrow will bring, step out on faith and place your feet on an angel's wing.
Your yesterdays and today, have brought you much hurt and sorrow, be not afraid of what has not yet been seen, for your time is borrowed.

Surely each day that you live will bring about anew, and be not afraid of that which you can't see, you're not suppose too.
If God placed it all before you and allowed you to see, then how would you know of a thing called faith and what He meant for it to be?

Surely, everything that you once believed in, to be true was without fear or doubt because you simply thought you knew.
At least that's what the world would have you to believe, despite those times when you grieved, being afraid was something you couldn't conceive.

Not knowing there would come a time when you would be put to the test, you stress and pondered regret, unwilling to take the next step.
Any old excuse will do, as you search to find a reason why, so afraid that you'll fail, when really all you have to do is try.

No one or thing should ever hold you back from trying, you hold the key to your tomorrows why keep denying.
Sieze the moment and not the opportunity of what has been given, for truly God has allowed you a second chance to start living.

Because for so long you merely existed for the sake of trying, turn not away from the truth and accept what the Lord is supplying.
Now that you stand before the world alone, faced with a life changing decision, be not afraid because you can't see what the Lord has envisioned.

Be not afraid of that which the Lord has placed before you, it's your just reward; so keep the faith because there's much more in store for you.

Fragile Heart

To look at you from an outward perspective, one can't see what's inside, which can be deceptive.
Strong yet weak from the years of pain and hurt, and despite the strain and pressure it's amazing you still work.

Never missing a beat as you go about your day, even when you are consumed by what others may say.
Being of strong will and determination your mission is to survive; yet your emotions and feelings hinder you from inside.

That's not a bad thing it's just the wrong thing to do, when you consider all the things God has set before you.
It's hard to conceive when all you do is grieve, at some point in life you simply have to believe.

Try looking beyond the fact of the matter, which made you sadder, and embrace the matter of facts and you'll become gladder.
Instead of analyzing the reason focus on the purpose behind it, and you'll find its meant to strengthen just don't quit.

The Lord knows as fragile as you are, this time is given to heal from the scars.
Unsure and uncomfortable at times you feel so strange, just relax and be patient Christ is about to make a change.

Not to you but within you, it's you who made the request, so be not confused or dishearten by each and every test.
It's not going to be easy it was never meant to be, because fragile heart your soul cries out to be free.

You see it's no longer up to you so release and let go, for the powers that be has taken over the show.
The script is being rewritten each day you walk the face of this earth, and fragile heart somewhere along the way you'll realize your worth.

It may not be today or even come tomorrow it's all according to the Lord when He will put an end to your sorrow.
Truly it's not as bad as you think it is only a phase, just remain meek and humble fragile heart and give Him the praise.

Just understand and know all that you put in surely you will get out, for each day you live the Lord will strengthen your fragile heart beyond any doubt.

When Words Aren't Enough

Truly a time will come in your life when words are not needed to make things all right.
They say communication is the key, yet I have no words to express how much you mean to me.

Yes I tell you I love you and how much I care, but there are no words that soothe me as you're rubbing my hair.
We've learned at an early age to speak that which you feel, but God knows there are other ways of showing a deeper love still.

When words aren't enough!
Some seem to lose sight of that which has been given, for truly no words can describe the life I am now living.

With no words I show you through my emotions, and if there's any doubt look deep within my eyes and see my devotion.
A sweet caress or just a gentle touch, tells me more than any words of how you love me so much.

As we lay next to each other in such a sweet embrace, you need not say a word for it is written all over your face.
When words aren't enough!

It's not so much as what you say as it is what you show, as you've reached deep within and allowed me to grow.
Worth its weight in gold because it's a love so true, and if I had to tell the world no words could I choose.

It's not what one make as it is what one is willing to accept what it is, as love goes way beyond human emotions as it allows one to live.
With all that I have and all that you bring forth, God knows its unconditional love for mere words are not enough.

The Purpose

That which so many of us today struggle to define, not realizing the purpose for us all is not that hard to find.
We've yet to understand no matter how persistence, as so many are lost to the true nature of their existence.

Searching and wandering looking for the reason behind it, they see not the purpose, which throws them into an uncontrollable fit.
Knowing they have the ability and might to, they have yet to acknowledge the purpose of that which they now must go through.

Making all the right moves and doing the right thing, they fail to understand the purpose why they have yet to grasp the ring.
With so much love and understanding in their heart, they misinterpret the purpose of another's love right from the start.

Surely love will conquer all things and bring you peace, yet they become unaware of its true purpose as it brings them to disbelief.
The purpose is not for us to see yet to experience, as we have often become complacent thus there is a need for interference.

It's not meant to be pleasant or easy to overcome, because so often when we are faced with it we choose to run.
Not toward it head on full of conviction like we should, but away from it because we have doubt that we could.

Not realizing that if we would, we have a better sense and understanding of that which we misunderstood.
Some times it's as plain as the nose on our face, yet we'd rather ignore not knowing it's the right time and place.

*J*ust where God wanted us to be in order to see, the purpose and the reason not according to the world and that's what He wants us to believe.
Standing still, for it not your will but His that it shall be done, and that purpose is to prepare you for that day when you won't be able to run.

*W*here you can't hide, when all things shall be revealed, that the purpose was to insure and let us know that nothing can be concealed.
By His might and not by our sight, because He knows some of us have yet to get it right.

*S*o look not for any explanations as only the facts remain, that life was given unto us and each purpose draws you closer to His holy name.

One Day

As life would have it there are some things we've yet to understand, and no matter how hard we try some of us still don't comprehend.
Basing our thoughts and comprehension on what is portrayed by others, that we can't see pass yesterday and recognizes our true sisters and brothers.

Yes, it's hard to imagine that such a person does exist, but one day they will cross your path and no longer will they be a myth.
Of all the stories you were told about how a person can be that you find it hard to believe in the one you now see.

As questions run through your mind there has to be a flaw, so you look pass the truth and reflect upon your scars.
Holding on to a distant memory or maybe a bad situation, that one you prayed for one day has come this day without reservations.

Because what he or she is willing to share is unconditional with no strings, and despite what you've felt it's all about the mental and the joy it brings.
Yet day after day we want to compare them to what was, for fear of what we don't understand and not realize it simply because of.

Your yesterday are forever in the back of your mind, and you miss the realness of them being kind, thus you feel you've yet to find.
Because one day you hoped and you know one day you will, be blessed with such a person that surely will fulfill.

Where you are able to look pass the physical and know such a thing exist, and understand the true nature of such a special gift.
You then realize it's not that hard to imagine what God had in mind, as you'll forget about your pass and look forward to a better time.

Woke Up One Morning

I woke up one morning and found myself struggling to make sense, as all my thoughts and decisions had me straddling the fence.
It was like all that once was, was not for me at all, truly I had been awaken to something special yet I couldn't recall.

If you asked me what it was no answer could I give, all I can say is I no longer desired the life I once lived.
Thus I struggle to see my way through that from which I had awakened, and all I could do was pray to God and ask not to be forsaken.

The world as I knew it seemed so shallow and empty, because on that morning I awoke and the world was no longer in me.
Despite the love I once had and the friends I once knew, I felt something inside of me that touched me through and through.

It truly was something they would never have understood, because for me that morning was the first time I really stood.
Not on my own but by that which I now see, and despite them feeling I am being selfish I've got to do it for me.

The world we once shared has run its course, and God knows my heart is filled with much remorse.
I can't turn away from that which awakened me that morning, as each day that I am alive I am blessed with reassuring.

Yet the problem still remains as I struggle to make them understand, it's not their fault Christ just took hold of my hand.
It's no longer about what was for me because I've witnessed what is, and I've given all I can give, and now God knows I want to live.

Before I believed in what the world would have me to believe, but by the grace of God I now see things differently and now I must grieve.
As I once thought and believed that my life was perfect in every way, I now see it was according to the world and what others had to say.

So now comes the hurt, which truly is not my intent, but I must find the significant of that morning and what it represents.
And as I struggle with it all I realize one thing, that which I now go through only ensures that which Christ is about to bring.

Realizing I just didn't wake up that morning feeling that way, you see Jesus Christ woke me up and showed me what He was trying to say.

Chapter Two

Redefining Self

"Words of Growth"

On My Own

As I stand before the world in the midst of the storm, I am faced with reality, for truly I am on my own.
Afraid of the unknown I search to find peace of mind despite the wrong, because of all the things I've yearned peace is the one thing I've truly longed.

Thus I struggle to maintain a sense of dignity and some understanding, but there are times when it seems so hard because I can be so demanding.
Truly that which has befallen me is of my own doing, but I pray that God looks within my heart and forgives me for my choosing.

As I've felt so many times before there was something missing in my life, for I looked the other way when He was showing me what was right.
Trying to find a substitute for that which there truly was none, I now find my self on my own knowing there can only be One.

Seeking forgiveness and mercy I stand before Him on my own, because that's where He needed me to be if I am truly to move on.
Although I am on my own I'll never be alone, and despite how I may feel now I am blessed by what He has shown.

As I stand in the midst of it all I must not complain, because there are so many others who know not of such change.
They've yet to realize that all things of this world are for the moment, and to overcome each burden that one carries one truly must own it.

If I were to compare my being alone to theirs surely I would have some regret, as God has allowed me this time to kneel and confess.
Knowing that there are so many lost in this world by what they perceive, I am truly thankful for this time on my own; how else would I be able to believe.

*T*hus to be on my own and face this old world with fear, I cling to the promise that my Savior will always keep me near.
So fear not the unknown yet be patience, for that which is about to be shown, as each day is a blessing for you are not on your own.

Crossroads

Where the road we've traveled throughout life intersect with the road we envisioned hoping we'd get it right.
Looking back from whence we've come, knowing now that our life will never be the same.

Is it too late or have we run out of time, now that we are at the crossroads echo through our mind.
Thinking to ourselves if only we had the chance, there would be some thing we'd do differently to correct our stance.

The heart is heavy as our mistakes along the way reappear; unable to see in any directions we are overcome by fear.
Knowing in our heart that we can no longer live this way, we find our selves at the crossroads wondering how to pray.

Looking for the right words that once came with such ease, there truly are no words to express just how we really feel.
All that we know is that our life is now in shambles, and now that we are at the crossroads all we seem to do is ramble.

Not knowing the cause but in reality we really do, as we are now face to face with the truth not knowing if we'll make it through.
Surely there's no turning back for we've come too far, but here we are at the crossroads unable to hide the scars.

Exposed before the whole world we feel so a shame, wishing we could turn back the clock or some how rearrange.
Wishing it all were a dream and when we awake it would be gone, but that will never happen knowing we have to pay for our wrong.

*O*vercome with fear we search to understand faith, because now that we are at the crossroads we see all our mistakes.
Crying out to the heavens yet we failed to shed a tear, and find our selves asking God to forgive us hoping He will hear.

*I*s it too late, have we gone pass the point of no return, and then we hear a voice say from this point on everything you must earn.
There is a price to pay and it may cost you your life, as your soul cries out for mercy wanting you to get it right.

*S*tanding at the crossroads not knowing whether to go left or right, you fall down on your knees and call out to Jesus Christ.

Each Day

None shall be perfect thus we are given each day according to God's will, thus we must be thankful for them all and strive each day to fulfill.
As joy does come in the morning, and each day we are blessed by what He is showing.

Each day that we are given, He truly is pleased, thus our work for that day is worthy despite when we might grieve.
Some live their today's as if it where their last, while others chose to live their life according to each day knowing it soon will pass.

As each day that passes insures and guarantees of a better tomorrow, knowing there will come a tomorrow built on a guarantee of no more sorrow.
It's the work that one does and not the job where they labor that has so many confused and unable to savor.

Troubled by all the things that one has to do, we forget about that which we are supposed too.
Each day is but a lesson taught from up above, yet there are those who fail to appreciate that unconditional love.

One day at a time that's all one can hope for, so why look beyond today and miss the glory so often ignored.
Each day that we live require our confessing, although we are not perfect we shall not be move because of our testing.

Despite those days when things seem not to go right, we understand the true purpose of that day and try to live it right.
As our feelings are formed in our mind and not from the heart, thus we stand not by sight but by faith for each day is a new start.

*L*iving on a wing and a prayer we must embrace each day, and not live our life according to what others wish to portray.
Surely each day brings us that much closer to reality, and it's not all about the mentality but your spirituality.

*N*othing is further from the truth despite what others may say, just live each day and for the others you just pray.

Finding My Way

Throughout my journey across this barren land, I search to find my way and fully understand.
For so long it's always been what mankind would have me to believe, yet I was never really happy or content with what I had received.

Looking at it all from another's perspective, I find myself pondering everything that I've now collected.
Yes I made it through the storm and I made it through the rain, but my physical strength has paid the price thus my soul is all that remains.

As I wander day to day I surely will find my way, as my journey takes me way beyond the mere words of what another may have to say.
What he or she may claim to be true and they are willing to profess; my journey leads me further away from them because my soul is all I have left.

Finding my way comes with a price yet I wouldn't hesitate to think twice, as my faith grows stronger each day, which replaces my physical, might.
Seeing that which was for what it really was, I no longer can follow in those footsteps simply because.

Each day I awaken I shed a part of the old to reestablish anew, even when those days are troublesome it's faith that brings me through.
I never claimed to be perfect although there were times I thought it, thus my journey to finding my way has taught me I must never quit.

You see finding my way was never about the finding, as much as it was about letting Jesus Christ do the refining.
Finding my way is about omission, based solely upon listening, as I now realize and hear what my ears have been missing.

The joyous sounds of life and the sweet echo of freedom, for in this land of plenty when it comes to Christ, you can't beat Him.

The melody is pure for surely it has been refined, and even though I've yet to reach my destination it's His love and mercy I am glad to have found.

Searching

*W*ith the world before me I set out to make a name for myself, and truly that which I search for shall not be placed upon a shelf.
I look not for fortune or fame, only that which is according to the holiest of names.

*I*t's not my concern to live like a king among the many, but to live like a pauper and be happy with just a few pennies.
For truly the struggle is worth its weight in gold, and when all is said and done I will be blessed with a wealth untold.

*S*o as I look I search not for the finer things in life, but search to no end to possess that, which defines my life.
Arrogance and self-indulgence will never hinder my steps, because in order to achieve that which I search for I must not think of only myself.

*K*nowing that which I yearn, one must be willing to pay the price, so I need not be in a hurry if I wish to get it right.
The journey to which I travel truly has many roads, and although I packed light I still will carry a heavy load.

*N*ot by my own admission but by my submission, because I realize that's what's needed if I am to succeed and enjoy what I envisioned.
I know not my fate nor do I have a crystal ball, but one thing is for certain throughout my quest I am supposed to fall.

*I*t doesn't mean I failed, only that I have yet to prevail, as each time is a lesson learned and a story I must be willing to tell.
Unlike so many others unwilling to give credit where credit is due, I know it is because of my searching Jesus Christ would see me through.

Despite what I thought He knew what was in my heart, and it would be through my searching that He would truly set me apart.
Not from those around me but the world in which I searched, and no matter the direction I choose I've come to realized it's suppose to hurt.

If it were not for the pain and the mass confusion, how could I ever hope to find that which I searched for and look past the illusion?

Where I Am

Certainly I may not be where I wish to be in my life, but I am thankful for where I am despite my strife.
Taking each day as it comes and accepting my fate, for I know in my heart it's only a matter of time thus I wait.

So often I try to look ahead and find myself wondering how, when I should be content with the way things are now.
Thus there would be no pressure or stress placed upon myself, and realize there will come a time for every thing else.

While so many others have pondered these same thoughts, as they look pass the very thing they so eagerly sought.
I am no better for I too have struggled with that same fear, wanting to see pass today and see tomorrow which isn't so clear.

Thus I look not beyond that which has been placed before me, because when I take a look back how could I not be grateful for what the Lord had for me.
It only took me a moment to understand and define just where I am in life and know I am doing just fine.

So often we become complacent by what we have and what we've got, that we think not to look back to a time when we were among the have not.
Realizing how much we've changed for the good and some bad, but I can only speak for myself, that where I am I truly am glad.

Not where I want to be, but blessed to have witnessed so much, and realize that I didn't make it on my own as I was never out of touch.
It was all according to God's plan to be just where I am, and as I look back I see the power and mercy of His almighty hand.

*P*icking me up and closing doors that needed not to be open, because reaching my destination of today is what I once was hoping.
Yet here I am just where He wanted me to be, and I ask Him now for forgiveness in my efforts to see beyond that which He has for me.

*B*ecause where I am signifies the person He knows I am, as I could never change where I am only improve upon who I am?
This is the process, something so many fail to see and understand, because despite where you are in the world it's who you are that's been molded by God's hands.

*S*o you see where I am is because God made me who I am, and despite where I may want to be I now cherish this life for truly it's grand.

Why Me?

As I stand in the midst of the storm I search to find my way, not knowing the true magnitude of it all I take time to pray.
With many unanswered question I search to find the reason, as I am determine to find the source, which is so displeasing.

But of all these questions "Why me?" is the one that plagues my mind, as I find myself repeating it time after time.
As I struggle to make sense I look for its pretence, because that which troubles me I have no defense.

Why me? Echo with in my very being, I find it hard to believe just what I am seeing.
Why me, for truly despite my wrongs I've done some good, thinking to myself I did all I could.

Why me? As I see so many others living so care free, taking two step forward and find things are further away from me.
Why me, when I've given to others as I had to go without, as those where the three step that set me back no doubt.

Why me? For surely I've put in my time to make things right; yet I find it very hard to fall asleep at night.
Then one morning I awoke ready to start my day, and I asked this question as I began to pray.

Not a selfish prayer but one with real concern, and I received my answer telling me I have yet to earn.
Because despite all that I considered to be just and worthy, I had yet to free myself from of all that which is considered worldly.

*T*hus I found the pretence to which there truly was no defense, and I realize that I had been straddling the fence.
Those echoes were to be my calling of what was to be, and now I realize I should have been saying why not me.

*M*y giving was from the heart as I did my best, but now I understand there will always be a test.
Thus my good was simply not good enough, as I had yet to establish a bond between faith and trust.

*N*ow all I can say is why not me, for who better to serve the Lord and know what it means to be free.
Why not me for surely I've yet to grow, and along the way understand the One whom I've come to know.

*W*hy not me, as I now stand patiently knowing it's not my time, and realize the question why me, is was what He wanted me to find.

The Path

With two roads before me, I traveled the one most taken, like so many others before me I was never forsaken.
It may have taken me a while to find this out, but the path I now walk I shall never have doubted.

The one I'd traveled was the one I decided to take, the path that now stands before me is the one where I can no longer perpetrate.
The path that once led me to no where I shall no longer fear for it has become the path that will take me way beyond here.

The one where my voice seemed to never have been heard has become the one where my heart expresses and speaks my every word.
I once would envision and imagine what the possibilities could be, and the one I now travel allows me that which is meant for me.

Because, before I would often stumble and fall, now no matter the situation all I have to do is just stand and call.
I now realize I am no longer lost and confused, it's just something I like so many others was simply not use to.

The path I was once on presented many obstacles causing my forgetfulness, so as I stand before the world I travel alone to seek salvation and righteousness.
Not for me as a whole yet for my soul, for truly one day I shall be made whole.

Knowing that I could never correct the wrongs that I've done, but the path I now walk will make me strong with each rising sun.
The path I once traveled truly was a never-ending abyss, and although the path now before me may end it will never cease to exist.

On Bending Knee

As I bow down before the Lord, I express my heart felt desire and to be on one accord.
Knowing that as my day begins I knelt down and prayed, and as my day now comes to a close I am blessed for what He gave.

Most gracious for the time allowed unto me, as I now look pass the worldly and like what I see.
It may not be what I had planned or even had in mind, but I remain humble knowing I live on borrowed time.

Despite my thoughts and feeling of where I want to be, I dare not take advantage of what is given unto me.
Even though I struggle to make sense and put things into perspective, it's on bending knee I seek to reach His objective.

To take what is given and learn to accept, and realize sometime my decisions aren't always correct.
It's human nature to want, driven by a desire to achieve, yet it's on bending knee I find one must wait in order to receive.

So as my day evolved it's according to His will, and if I am to find peace first I must stand still.
Regardless if it's not where I want to be at this stage it's truly what I asked for on bending knee as I prayed.

Thus a sacrifice is in order to obtain my rightful place, as it was on bending knee I gave my all to my Saving Grace.
Realizing, who am I to question or even doubt my progress, for truly each day that is given is only a test.

Whether I fail or succeed that's something I must face, just thankful it's on bending knee I asked for forgiveness when I become displaced.
If only for a moment I become consumed by a thought, I look to the heavens and realize I've given it more power than I ought.

So I take a brief second and reconnect with the Most High, and tell Him how thankful I am for being alive.
So as my day comes to a close and nightfall draws near, I reflect upon today and now see the purpose and the reason so clear.

You see it was on bending knee where I draw closer to Thee, and tonight before I fall asleep I am most gracious for what He has allowed me to see.

Chapter Three

Social Awareness

"Words of Knowledge"

There Was No Moses

There was a story told long ago about such a people and a place, where such a thing did exist and it was according to race.
Where the children of God were held in bondage never to be free, but it took a man name Moses to make the Pharaoh see.

That story has now come to life for those who search but have yet to find, and as I sit and think there was no Moses to ease their troubled mind.
With all that we have as a nation the power and the might, there is no leader among us to see that it gets done right.

Lost sheep with no shepherd to guide them along their way, they contemplate tomorrow not knowing if there will be a better day.
What was will no longer be, as God has made sure of that, and without a Moses they fail to understand there's no turning back.

Unable to look beyond that which was and see their blessing, they cling to the voice of mankind and what he is addressing.
How could such a thing happen for surely there is a God, yet they fail to realize that He and not mankind is in charge.

The writing was on the wall and its message was very clear, for truly time is at hand and ours is coming near
History is repeating itself by all that has come to pass and its funny how some think that this world is going to last.

He has scattered His children for a reason, let there be no misconceiving, for surely what was done was due to His displeasing.
With no Moses to turn to He would hope we would rely on one another, and for once look pass the color of ones skin for truly we all are brothers.

Yet there was no Moses up front to show the people out, as God took notice of those whom deem themselves worthy with all the clout.
Judge not for they too shall have to answer the call, for leaving His people in a wilderness of destruction and chaos to which we all were appalled.

Not of the devastation but by what mankind seemed unwilling to do, and because there was no Moses our people had no way of making it through.
Time is of essence and we hesitate not when it comes to war, yet we let time pass by when it came to God's children and that hurts to the core.

They say it's better late than never and we must rally for the cause, but what ever happened to our Moses now let us take a pause.

To The Messenger

Go before my children and speak the word, and fret not if it's something they've never heard.
Be like a gardener and plant a seed within their mind, and when you depart from them they'll know you are a special kind.

Go before my children and share the knowledge brought about through sacrifice, and help them understand it symbolizes wisdom and truth about this thing called life.
Knowing that mistakes have been made and despite it all you've always prayed, for there will come a time when they too shall look to be saved.

Share with them that which has caused you much grief, and in its own little way they too shall find relief.
Be not ashamed to express and show your most intimate feelings, because for you as well as them it allows healing.

Hold back not your tears for truly it will cleanse the soul, as it allows those around you to feel warmth in a world so cold.
Worry not about what they may think it's not worth the time, as you've become the messenger to deliver hope and understanding, undaunted and refined.

Never claiming to be perfect for surely you have your faults, but unlike them you understand the reasoning as it tugs at your heart.
Not knowing the outcome you continue on and grow, waiting for the moment when your flicker of light will start to glow.

Not so much as for the whole world to see, as it is for those to see and have a better understanding of what is to be.
Be not consumed by what may follow like fortune and fame, yet remain a humble servant for truly you've been ordained.

Not by what mankind or others may choose to label, but by the grace and power of Jesus Christ for truly He is able.

The Masterpiece

Constructed by a thought, implemented through determination, the masterpiece is formed by a true revelation.
Not of what the world would have one to believe, but by what one had to endure at those times when they would grieve.

As they've become a picture upon a canvas for the whole world to see, they left their life up to others interpretation of what truly was to be.
Not quite sure of how they were to represent themselves, they set out upon the world not fully knowing but truly were compelled.

Framed by a society, yet not knowing the cost of life, they live within the framework feeling everything is all right.
A treasured possession truly worth its weight in gold, they lived not knowing the true value of their existence, as it was never told.

Thus a misrepresentation portrayed throughout their canvas of life, letting their mind and not their heart be on display, as they stood beneath the light.
Hoping one day they would become a true masterpiece, they thought not of any security to protect them from thieves.

Then one day that which they valued was taken away without any reason, and now that which they were once told they now have a hard time believing.
Feeling the pain from each brush stroke that they placed upon their canvas, they've come to the realization it was because of the world and not He who commands it.

In the art gallery of life they find themselves placed in a dark room, with very little light feeling like a flower unable to bloom.
They search for an artist to reconstruct their portrait of life, and make them once again a pleasure to be beheld by another's sight.

*T*ruly they are rare and unique and possess a certain quality of life, because their beauty goes way beyond that which can be seen by any light.
Thus the artist picks up his brush and begins to refine each brush stroke, for his only intent is to restore and enhance the framework that was broke.

*N*ot so much as the portrait as it is the artwork within the frame, bringing out that which was hidden even though it may look the same.
Only to those who see through a naked eye, but the true beauty of the painting is what's inside.

*l*Not for the whole world to see but for those of us who believe, and truly marvel at his work knowing only he can conceive.
Such elegance of one true expression of what the portrait is suppose to be, that it's hard not to notice that it's his work we see.

*O*nes thoughts and understanding are no longer left up to another's interpretation, and the portrait now before us brings true revelation.
Not of what was but what is to be, as one stands before the art gallery of the world totally free, knowing no price can be placed upon His final masterpiece.

The Message

It's quite clear so listen here, there's no need to fear, just take a moment and lend me your ear.
The time won't be wasted and soon you'll understand my reasoning, to the message that awaits you, which is most pleasing.

Time is not lost nor has it passed you by, you just failed to understand the message as you sit there and cry.
The pain and hurt you feel on the inside came from a thought, and you never got the message because it was from within that you fought.

Taken what was done and not realizing what had been given, it was hard to comprehend the message that said don't stop living.
Because no matter the situation that caused you to fall, all you had to do was look up and see the message written on the wall.

Although it's hard to read due to the tears in your eyes, the message is clearly saying you are only half alive.
Caught in the middle of what was and what is to be, hold back not your tears and set your soul free.

Once you look past the pain and no longer see the hurt, you'll see the message more clearly, telling you it's all about your worth.

Portrait

I gaze at the portrait upon the wall in a gallery of life, reflecting all that is good and bad, full of success and strife.

Truly it is priceless for time has made sure of that, and as I sit and stare I realize it will never come back.

It speaks volume of a race destine to succeed, but somehow I now wonder if it's forever lost because of greed.

The originality it expresses makes my heart skip a beat, as it takes me back to a time oh so sweet.

Memory that forever stay on my mind has captivated my souls for it's deeply entwined.

With each brush stroke I see sacrifice and determination, overwhelmed tears begin to fall as we live in a world of total separation.

Each color so profound and vibrant it makes me proud, that we once had a voice which spoke out loud.

Within its artwork one can't help but to notice its sincerity, but as I look around today it seems to be a rarity.

I pay strict attention to its details for it signifies my history, thus instills a sense of purpose, honor and respect and most of all dignity.

Unlike the portrait of today framed in glitter and gold, I find peace and understanding within the frame of old.

Taking me back, which give me strength to move ahead, for I remain humble and remember those who are now dead.

You see the portrait on the wall is a picture that many have forgot, because they were to busy trying to reach the top.

Once Upon A Time

I could start off by telling a story but would you believe it, or would you feel it's out dated and not understand it.
Surely the times have changed and people seem to have a new attitude, and often when one talks about the past they somehow come unglued.

So I'll take my time as I hope not to offend, but I must speak about the past and be true to myself and not pretend.
We all know the history of how a nation was forged through blood, sweat and tears, and now our youth of today take it for granted and set us back four hundred years.

Do you remember the saying about the "village raising a child," well the village still exists but the child is in the street running wild?
There once was a time when structure and foundation was secure and now it seems as if the foundation and structure is unsure.

As society now dictates and so many follow suit, it's like "once upon a time" never existed and no one knows the truth.
What once was seems to have been lost and a forgotten past, and the roots of our heritage are in need of cultivating if we truly are to last.

Respect was the soil, and dignity was the water that quenched the thirst, and it seems today it's taken a back seat and we wonder if it will get worse.
Honor was the very fiber that was used to sew and keep the family together, and now some do it own their own and are unconscious of the stormy weather.

Many lying to themselves saying they won't do as their parents did, but back in the day you were made to know that you were a kid.
I am going to give mine that which I didn't have coming up then, but you forgot to give the one thing that now seems to bring their life to an erupt end.

Because despite all that you didn't have your life was grand, unlike today no matter what you give they have the nerve to want to get up and stand.
Taking it upon them as if they know and forget the old school, but once upon a time we were told, don't grow to be no fool.

You see once upon a time people live with a purpose, and now today we live for the material and that's what really hurts us.
So who's to blame, is it society or is it the changing of time, well here's a little something I wish to rest upon your mind.

The time has not changed, each hour of the day and year is the same, you see it's the people who have changed and forgotten Jesus Christ's name.

Our Covenant

We as a people must come together for the benefit of our color, and form an alliance on the truth and renew our trust among one another.
You see I heard it from a brother talking to another, as he was putting together a covenant hoping we would advance a little further.

Despite the struggle and the inequality we all face, we no longer can continue to leave it up to another race.
A point well spoken as we all bear witness to the destruction, because when you add it all up we've become the deduction.

After much thought and consideration I envisioned what he was showing, and God placed these words on my heart as I composed this poem.
It's not so much about what the covenant should be about, as it is something we as a people must think about before we're left out.

We can't live together because for so long we were forced to live apart, and we've yet to realize the pain and that saddens my heart.
Let's stop competing with the haves and have nots, and come together for God knows we are all we've got.

That which was forged some time ago still exists today, and until we free our minds things will continue to happen this way.
Four hundred years have passed and we've yet to reach our potential, thus our covenant is such that we shed some light on the obvious and that's our mental.

You see not knowing means we're not growing, because we are to busy flowing that we pay no attention to what the other is showing.
Thus our covenant must be constructed within our minds right from the start, and as we reach out to one another let our words come from the heart.

Because that which comes from within surely has a place in the world today, as God knows it's been missing as we see by what others display. It's as much our fault as it is theirs because we forgot to believe in the spirituality and the wisdom that Malcolm and Martin taught.

So the time is at hand for us as a people to understand, that in order for us to stand we must come together and devise a plan.
We have the means and the resources it's really not that hard, but if we are to succeed as a people we must first seek God.

Not Forsaken

To my people lost and bewildered in the struggle of life, all is not lost just place your trust in Jesus Christ.
No one fully knows of that which you now go through, for you truly are among the blessed ones who have a chance to start anew.

Be not mislead by the thought of it was a force of nature, because it's all according to the will and power of God who created you.
For surely you've often wondered what this world was coming to, well He just sent a reminder and believe me He's not through.

Testing the will of those whom He deemed as His child, and setting an example for others who cared not to try.
All is not lost only the material things you cherish most, but there comes a time in all our lives when we have to give up everything to receive the Holy Ghost.

Many lives have been lost and yet so many lives remain, only time and prayer will heal the wounds just remember only God can.
Just know this you have not been forsaken, for the writing is on the wall and it's time we all awaken.

Not to the destruction and chaos of all that was taken, but to the power of our God who has not forsaken.
As you've been granted another day despite your trials and tribulations, He's just bringing us all closer to the writing of the book of Revelation.

It's a test of our will as a people for truly we all are shaken, thus we must all come together and let not one be forsaken.
There is no mistaken to what our God is demonstrating, as it has become our defining hour for there are no words for justification.

Speak not of what is but translate one's voice into action, and let not be from your heart but from the soul and feel the satisfaction.
Not for the sake of but because of love, let it be of compassion and your desire to help another rise above.

They are the chosen ones and this we all must understand, for God had a plan and with the touch of His hand brought confirmation to our land. That it must take man to understand, that which was taken for granted, is of little value when it comes to the soul for truly He commands it.

Chapter Four

Unbeknownst to You

"Words of Healing"

Heroes

*T*hought of as a person who does something way beyond comprehension, as it takes a special person to do that as so many often mention.
Often times one has a split second to make a decision, not knowing what awaits them as he or she could never envision.
Surely we as humans have to wonder, what makes one do when there are at least over a hundred.

*I*f we were to look upon the masses we'd see they come in all colors, so tell me what makes them different from any other.
There will come a time when we all will be put to the test, and all that one can do is to give it their best.
Yet we idolize those who do and paint them bigger than life, but what about the single mother doing it on her on and getting it right.

*S*he's not looking for any ticker tape parade, she's just thankful for food and shelter and all her bills are paid.
The sad part is those whom we place on a pedestal are only human, and we immortalize them while other lives are being ruined.
The heroes of war take center stage, to take our minds off the tragedy of lives lost and the mistakes that were made.

*B*ecause it's about the hero and our desire to acknowledge, and have no time for the child left behind who had dreams of going to college.
Lost in a world of the abyss, failed by the system he balls up his fist, and lashes out at his own race because of something he missed.
Yet we continue to honor our heroes and fallen comrades, while the kids in our street are fighting for something they'll never have.

*D*on't get me wrong taking nothing away from anyone who does good, It's when you place them above everyone else for something that we all should.
Maybe it's just me but it seems that we've lost focus, but there was truly

one hero that came to mind as I wrote this.
And upon further thought and consideration I've misspelled the word, you see because He defines the word through and through because *HE ROSE.*

In Your World

How can I express the way I truly feel, when you live in a world where reality is not real?
If I were to share my thoughts worthy of conversation, would the world you live in allow you to speak without any reservation?
Letting each word that I speak take hold and be accepted or would the world you live in think it was all a deception.

Could I or should I try to explain that which I truly believe, or would the world you live in some how make you feel I was trying to deceive.
Even though I clearly understand the nature of what's being said, I wonder if the world you live in would allow you to see it and not be mad.
Because in your world there exist much anger and disappointment, and despite what I've said and done there is still no enjoyment.

In your world you only see that which others portray as real, and regardless of my efforts you refuse to allow yourself to feel.
Not knowing that in your world there's no room for you to heal, but I refuse to be the one who turns their back thus I kneel.
Knowing that in your world you find it hard to believe it's true, thus I pray to God that He gives you the strength to make it through.

Try as you may and try, as you will, nothing will ever change in your world until you take time and stand still.
If only for a moment if only for a second, and realize it is because of your world that you are affected.
It's not by choice nor is it, as we say, by chance that you've now succumbed, and you never realized what God was trying to achieve despite what your world has done.

Yet so many take it to heart and fall off into a thing called depression, and never step beyond their world to look in another direction.
It's self-evident for surely it shows on their face, because in your world no one ever thinks of their Saving Grace.

Thus you knew not the time or the place when your world fell apart, and never thought for a moment that God had plans for you right from the start.

You see in order to, one simply must be willing to go through, only then will the reason become clear because in your world you had no clue.

So Unforgiving

Tell me who among us is perfect surely not I, here's a little revelation about letting go of what you feel inside.
We have our sticking points to where we refuse to budge, and if someone were to cross that line you feel it was because. They didn't care or they where just thinking of them self, because the pain and sorrow they caused makes you feel there is nothing left.

Surely you made it clear right from the start, and some how you can never forgive them as it tugs at your heart.
You hold onto the pain and become content just grieving, not knowing that you are denying yourself to understand the true reason.
Life's too short to be held down by that which you have no control, and yes a mistake was made but why deny your self a moment to be consoled.

So many today won't forgive and let go of the moment, until they make them pay when they've already owned it.
Human nature is what is yet some take it to the extreme, so unforgiving that we are unable to wipe our own slate clean.
The smallest of things can and are measured beyond its scope because you've become so unforgiving that another simply has no hope.

Regardless of what he or she does to try and mend the damage, you're so unforgiving that you no longer ask; you simply demand it.
Unable to realize that he or she may hurt more than you, it doesn't matter to you because you're so unforgiving without a clue.
Well here's one for those who don't and I hope you understand, when you become so unforgiving you go against God and not the woman or man.

Do you realize the precious time that you let slip away, you see if he were so unforgiving then surely we would have no need to pray.
What He has placed before you is but a test of your will, but during that

time you never called upon Him to help you heal.
And I know some of you did but resentment filled your heart, for truly if you were so unforgiving you would understand His part.

𝓕irst you must accept then take time to reflect, and if you feel it's worth your time then simply redirect.
Your thoughts and understanding of why it happened that way, and look deep within your self and remember what Jesus Christ had to say.

Owe You Nothing

My sisters and brothers we've all heard the stories, but we've failed to see the misconception but there is no need to worry,
At first it's hard to see thus we find it hard to believe, that neither the world nor those in it owe us anything because we have to grieve.

Yes believe it -- the world owes you nothing, because that which has befallen you is the price you pay for wanting.
Yet some feel because of another they simply deserve, but the truth be told that which another may have for you is reserved.

Not because you say it's so, but frankly because the other knows and in time it will show.
Yet they still feel it's owed because of their misfortune and grief, and end up doubting the very one to which they should have some belief.

It's not for you or I to stand in lieu of, what was portrayed by mistrust or a misconception of a thing called love.
What we've had to endure was reestablished as trust, not in one another but in the Almighty whom we owe so much.

Just because you were treated a certain way, it was by your own omission, thus another should not have to bow down to your submission.
The world owes you nothing, so what if you came up hard, if you made it this far then you owe it all to God.

Thus the payment you seek truly is the one you owe, and contrary to opinion it's something you will never out grow.
No amount of money or stature will suffice for what you truly owe, because until you've paid for the life that was given you really won't know.

Those years you had to go without, are the years you paid for living in doubt.
Not for what you know but for what you thought you did know, and that's why you lived your life in a world feeling it was you who is owed.
Never considering the facts that it was you who was content with your decision, blind to what the Lord had to offer because of your worldly vision.

Thus neither I, nor the next one you meet will pay the price set forth by you, as we've already had to pay the price for that which we had to go through.
So despite what you think you are owed it's not our mission to share your load that which you carry you have yet to unload, and that's why you feel you are owed.

We all must pay a price for this thing called life, and what we owe is paid through strife, and until you realize you'll never be comfortable paying the price.
Doubt me not because you don't see things, as I do, just know it is because of Jesus Christ that I am able to see through.

Writing on the Wall

Truly my people the writing is on the wall, it's a shame some don't realize how close we are to the last trumpet call.
Nation rising up against nation because of mankind's ambitious nature, that they have no room in the heart for the One and only Creator.

What transpires within this world today is of man's design, and the Lord has revealed unto us that some will be left behind.
Yet with all that has happened and is still yet to come, more and more are traveling that much further away from the Holy Son.

We've got brothers turning against brothers and their sisters, children being brought up in a world having no respect for Mrs. or Mister.
They take the life of another without blinking an eye, with no conscious, as they believe it's a means to survive.

We see it more and more each day the writing is truly on the wall, but for some ungodly reason it's doesn't affect them at all.
Truly our days are numbered and it's only a matter of time, before the lost seek refuge lets just pray it's something they find.

The writing is on the wall as we see the righteous have gone astray, teaching and preaching the word but live their life a different way.
They are the shepherds tending and leading the flock toward salvation, and yet they themselves have fallen into temptation.

And if we as Christians feel that it doesn't affect us at all, then we've ignored the signs as well for truly the writing is on the wall.
Therefore we must all come together and set it straight, and despite the writing on the wall our faith in God tells us it's never to late.

Seasons extend over into season and we're still chasing time, the writing is on the wall as the Lord said it would do you remember that line, The writing is on the wall and man can no longer predict the weather, and regardless of the technology he's not that clever.

Thus the writing is on the wall and whether you can read or not, we need to get our life in order and seek Christ for He is all we've got.

The Street Talks

As the conservation is endless for that which it speaks goes unheard, and for as much as they have to say we hear not a word.
Knowing that their time is endless for they've withstood the test of time, and they have many stories to tell of those who didn't fair so fine.

Yet their voice goes unnoticed as others choose to speak for them, telling others about the street like it's their friend.
Truly they know not of the street only that which they portray, because if they listened to the street they wouldn't continue to live that way.

They have street smarts but the streets done something they'll never do, see despite where it is it has the ability to reach beyond those without a clue.
It's words of wisdom and understanding are over shadowed by others word's courage, as many lives are lost they pretend as if they are not worried.

You see the street knows it belongs to everyone but none shall claim, telling those who try it's a never-ending cycle with no fortune or fame.
Year after year it bears witness to the destruction of a people, claiming to be hard, strong and resourceful while all along they get weaker.

It speaks of those who tried in the past, yet no one is listening to figure out that's why they didn't last.
The street talks yet there are those who act like it doesn't exist; only if they would listen they'd understand the realness of the friends they now miss.

It talks about the many years of horror and dismay, and despite its best efforts, it falls on deaf ears as it sees the games they continue to play.
Trying to explain all the years of heartache and pain, to those who would listen, but it's often too late as it forgets their name.

The street truly has no enemies for it is a friend to all, it just wonders when will they ever listen and heed its call.
That which it has to offer has truly been over looked, because with all the stories it speaks of one could write a book.

The street holds not all the answers and the street has no cures, it's only a means of direction in ones life and he or she has to choose.
Ask yourself if the streets could talk would you really listen, well I am sorry to say it has and it's you who never hear a word; too busy whistling.
You see it wants to remind us all that hell is something we create, as we try to walk the streets proudly forgetting that God knows we only perpetrate.

The Will

It's one thing we as humans possess; yet we fail to obtain it's full potential due to a thing call stress.
Could it be because we haven't understood its true nature that exists, or is it because we misuse it to obtain that which we wish?

We are of strong will when it comes to that which we want, thus we are willing to push everything aside as to be so blunt.
Knowing that which we want and what we desire brings out the best of us for it ignites a fire.

Not realizing that another side of us is shown; despite all our pleasantries others bear witness to a side they've never known.
Your will to succeed and your will to survive, often is overshadowed by ones will to conquer than to simply stay alive.

To succeed some say is human nature, but often in the process some forget just who created us.
Truly all things are within our grasps, but the will of so many is to obtain it fast.
Our will to survive has taken on a whole new meaning for some, as they have missed the true meaning of a will wanting not to walk but run.

Life is but a game and to survive one must be of strong will, not realizing that life goes much deeper only if they were able to feel.
And unbeknown to them their will has led them beyond that which is real, because it's not of the world that any of us have the will.

We all have the will to do, yet we fail to understand the rules, you see God's true purpose of will is something we all must choose.
It's oh so easy when it comes to things of the world, but to leave it all behind and step out on faith some of us are not that thorough.

For our will is such that we feel we don't have the strength, and God has given us the power for that's what your will represents.
Yes the life you've come to know has tested your will you see it's all according to His plan *TO TEST YOU DEEPER STILL.*

The Gardner

He goes about his day oblivious to some, and those whom he tends to are thankful that he did come.
Tilling the soil and fertilizing the land to insure their roots, he walks every so lightly he has no need for boots.

Preparing for the upcoming harvest he carefully plants the seeds knowing it will be only a matter of time before they take heed.
Despite his best efforts he realizes some will never bear fruit, but he tends to them just the same despite their wayward roots.

Knowing as they begin to take shape will be the crucial stage he takes the time to cultivate that which he's made.
Will they grow to their fullest potential is his only concern, but if they are to bear fruit then it something they must earn.

He'll do His part to ensure they receive proper light; it's truly up to them whether or not they grow up right.
He never plants out of season thus there never is a mistake, as each plant is worthy of bringing forth food for the plate.

Some less than others but he doesn't discard their worth, he continues to shower them with water to enrich the earth.
It is their lifeline for without it they would parish, knowing one day they too will be among the fairest.

Each shall have the stone removed in order for them to grow, and he will pluck away the dead leaves, as they get old.
As they have yet to reach their full potential he keeps a watchful eye, as they will one day bear fruit and thus they begin to come alive.

But until then he will do his very best to ensure their growth, as one will not out grow the other and have time to boast.
Because within this garden there are many plants putting forth fruit, and as fate would have it some have forgotten their roots.

Thus the gardener knows, and sees those plants have taken shape, and with the touch of his hand he can remove that which tries to pollinate.
Truly it is the life of every plant that remains his main concern, but truly to grow in his garden it is something every plant must earn.
There are many secrets to his garden to behold by so many, which will allow every plant to rise up and bring fruit a plenty.

The Reason Why

That which we search for yet it's often hard to find, with so many unanswered questions one could lose their mind.
Try as we may and try as we sometimes do, it would seem there has to be a reason why we have to go through.

Stuck in the moment we let it take control, and often we forget the very things we were told.
Somehow those words seemed to have slipped our mind, forgetting that they hold the key if we would only unwind.

So focus on the situation that we just can't let go, not knowing that if we did the reason why would surely show.
Yet we refuse to face the truth because of a thing called pride, feeling there has to be another or better reason why.

So the heartache begins and the sleepless nights are never ending, trying to hide behind it all fighting what doesn't need defending.
Fighting a battle with something that truly has no merit, we place it around our shoulders when its not meant for us to wear it.

Struggling from within to find out why it doesn't fit, we become unwilling to the reason and the why won't let us quit.
Only if we would understand the reason without adding the why, we'd know the cause and the purpose brought about by He who sits on high.

Just because we do or want doesn't make it's so and thus the reason and the why is what He is trying to show.
Not because of you, yet the things we continue to do and the reason why is because God's not through.

We had our chance and now it's all left up to Him, and the reason why is because of all our sins.
Whoever is without let them cast the first stone, and the reason why is because you thought you could do it on your own.

Pointing the finger and playing the name game and the reason why is because you forgot His name.
Not willing to concede you strive to achieve in haste and the reason why it's according to His time and place.
Feeling deep inside that there is something truly missing, and the reason why is because you refuse to listen.
Now do you remember those sacred words you were told, no matter what you do in life the reason why is because God's in control.

Chapter Five

SHE SPEAKS

"Words From Her Heart"

Reflection of my Dreams

To my daughter I thank you, as there are no words to describe, my love and affection for you that I feel deep inside.
I love all my children and not wanting to take anything from the other, you are my reflection and you've lived my dream despite my struggle.

As I take time to reflect upon how my life once was, I wouldn't have changed a thing seeing how you've grown because of.
My dreams were as such because I loved you so much, thus I've always wanted the best for you, as I could never do enough.

You've become the woman that I dreamed you would be, and it makes my heart happy for I see my reflection inside of thee.
There's no greater joy that any mother could ask for, as I've witnessed your success and achievement as you strive to accomplish much more.

The dreams I've envisioned are now reality as you've brought them to light, and I truly give honor to the Almighty for answering my prayers each and every night.
Not that you would get it right but to give you the strength and courage, and I can say without a doubt I was never worried.

Okay maybe a little but that's something mothers do, and as you embark upon motherhood I'll be there to see you through.
They say some parents try to live their life through their child, but in all honesty my darling you are my dream that keeps me alive.

As everyday brings anew and a reflection of my dreams comes shinning through, you've become that woman of elegance and truthfulness that I always knew.
When I speak of you to others I can't help but to smile, because I am so proud of your commitment and determination to finish every mile.

As the road to your success was truly not paved in gold, but as a mother I tried to instill in you the riches of a wealth untold.
Not by the world standards but by that which the Lord shall provide, thus you've become the reflection of my dream knowing it was only a matter of time.

There was need for pushing or shoving, for if you were to succeed all you would need was your mothers loving.
This poem comes from the heart for a love truly like no other, and it's all about you not taking anything away from your sisters and brothers.
Because a mother's love has the ability to reach out and console, I just wanted to take this time to express my love for you as you are the dream of my very soul.

In Her Rage

She knows not the answer, yet struggles to find one, trying to make sense of her anger with each rising sun.
With all that the world has placed at her feet, in her rage she finds it hard to fall asleep.

In her rage you only see her as an angry black woman, but fail to recognize her disappointment of lives being ruined.
In her rage you notice her bitterness and resentment toward man, but you never focus on the reason because it something you can't comprehend.

In her rage lie many years of hurt and pain, as she has witnessed and experienced heartache time and time again.
In her rage there are many doors that seem to have closed, and yet each day she awakens she asks of God to open just one more.

In her rage she prays when there will come a time, when some one will understand it's not because of man yet mankind.
In her rage she often expresses but her words go unheard, as they are over shadowed by her anger and not her encouraging words.

In her rage she fights to stay afloat in the midst of what she sees, knowing the power of God is the only thing, which will calm the turbulent seas.
In her rage she battles a never-ending barrage of thoughtlessness, as her heart yearns and her souls cries out for true righteousness.

Because you see in her rage there does exist such a thing called peace, and surely you wouldn't know it as you sit in disbelief.
In her rage some see it as envy and jealousy but within lie a passion and desire wanting others to simply believe.

In her rage she holds no animosity toward any one person, knowing that life's too short but wonders why others keep rehearsing.
Perpetrating life by what they see and what's done, it is within her rage she wishes to express that all in life is not fun.

And as much as she would like to rewrite the page, she continues to learn and trust in the Lord in her rage.
In her rage she explodes, fueled by hidden emotions as she wonders why others aren't aware and see pass the commotion.

In her rage she knows she's entitled, that's her right, thus she shall remain that strong black woman unwilling to give up the fight.
Not lost in obscurity nor hidden because of her race, in her rage she stands before the world hoping you never forget her face.

Her Dreams

Her dreams are as such that she need not fear for they shall never become a nightmare as Christ holds her near.
Living in a world with much mass confusion, she places her trust in Him and not the worldly illusion.

Thus her dream is of life not based upon a thought of reality, but living a life built on more than what the eyes can see.
Knowing that sometimes it can be deceiving, she relies on her faith and just keeps on believing.

That her dream is not a fantasy thus she need not fantasize, she stays true to her dream and looks beyond the world and truly realizes.
Very conscious of others who've lost sight of reality being real, she understands that her dream can become a reality as long as she remembers to kneel.

Often she reminisces of her friends dream turning into a nightmare, as she has a vision of her in a coffin much too her despair.
She has a vision of what her life could have been, knowing she met the wrong man oh how she misses her friend.

Thus she dreams not of the perfect man, but of one who simply understands, the woman who stands before him only God can command.
No knight in shining armor but one worthy of being a prince, relying on the Lord for his armor as he stands in her defense.

Humble not arrogant, secure and not confident in himself, yet the ability to stimulate the mind with love when there is nothing left.
One who looks past the physical to embrace the spiritual being, truly play the biggest part of that man she is dreaming.

Knowing the outer beauty one day will fade away, but the inner beauty shall always remain the focus from day-to-day.
And every night before she lies down to sleep, she thanks the Lord for a dream so sweet.
Knowing her dreams have become something she truly must earn, thus she can never be consumed by that which she may yearn.

Her First Step

To finally come of age and reflect upon her life, she has taken the first step toward healing and put an end to strife.
Not lost, but confused about the many things that affected her, she's begun to see more clearly through that which once was a blur.

Although hesitant to express what she truly feels, she found strength and courage, which allow her to heal.
Thus she's taken the first step to which there is no turning back, and unlike before she now understands the reasoning and vows to stay on track.

Like so many others before she's lived within a system, taking nothing or no one for granted, as she was once a victim.
Lost at love and lost a love that cannot be replaced, she walks no longer in the shadows as she found the love of her Saving Grace.

Tears of sadness are washed away by tears of joy and salvation, because her first step was out on faith and the second was taken without reservation.
Although her steps are not so clear she has no fear, because in her heart she knows each steps brings her near.

As she finds her self on her own so far away from home, she realizes her first step has taken her to a place where's she is never alone.
No longer weary or feeling she has no time to rest, she is thankful unto the Lord as He has allowed her to take a breath.

Knowing that it's more than just the act of breathing, as it allows her now to release and finally start believing.
That although she may be battered and bruised she's no longer confused, as she has taken the first step toward a life she never knew.

What does the future hold is truly not her concern, she lives one day at a time and that which she receives she truly has earned.
Realizing that what ever lies or stands in her way, is not her battle to fight she'll just kneel down and pray.

And of all the pleasure in the world to behold, nothing is more rewarding than her achieving her ultimate goal.
Not that of fortune or that of fame, but that which is truly given in Jesus name.

What She Is

*I*n this day and age we brothers of color have yet to discover, the true nature of our significant other.
What she is and what we expect her to be has been the demise of us all and I pray in time we'll see.

*Y*et we feel time is always on our side because there is no doubt, but if we only looked a little closer we'd understand what she really is about.
Often times we as men take the easier route, and when we are faced with the trueness of her we pause with doubt.

*N*ot fully understanding our role as we have lost sight, you see taking the easy route has taken us away from the light.
Well there is no book written nor is there a master plan, thus we have to make the conscious effort to maintain hold of her hand.

*B*ut fate would have it so that some fall short and wonder why, when all it took was taking the time before she started to cry.
We believe that first impressions are the focus and stability, but often time we sell our self-short and there lies the liability.

*I*t centers on taking the easy route to get those whom you pursue, not knowing a time will arise when you'll face the one who has a clue.
She might not know it all and she may not be a wiz, but one thing is for sure you can bet she knows what she is.

*S*o before you go off half cock and call her out of her name, check yourself and don't disrespect yourself because she won't play the game.
Yes it worked before and that's not a discredit to all women, but there are some out there who are content just swimming.

Never reaching land and never have a foothold on life, but when all is said and done, believe me there are those who are worthy of being a wife.
Yes she's independent for truly she's earned that right, she doesn't depend, so she need not defend, in order for you to see the light.

What she is, is a woman forged from the rib of man, and despite what you think of all women, there are those who embrace a more loving hand.
Not that of man but what he must represents, and for those of us who still wonder, look to the Heavens and I pray you see God's true intent.

To My Daughter

Where do I begin, for mere words aren't enough, but when all is said and done I hope you realize that I love you so much?
From the first day of knowing about your conception, I knew my life was headed in another direction.
It wasn't going to be easy but I never gave up hope, as God has truly blessed me with a precious gift more precious than any word ever wrote.

As you came into this world I wept tears of joy, and as I held you in my arms I vowed to you never would I ignore.
From that day forth I've stayed the course, and I am proud to say to you my daughter I have no remorse.
Each day was a blessing and our love withstood the test of time, and to this day there's nothing I wouldn't do for a daughter of mine.

Yes the road was bumpy and God knows we've encountered our share, of disagreements of opinion but there was never a moment when I didn't care.
Those times when you thought I was just being mean was my way of protecting you from the things you had not seen.
Knowing it was hard for you to see that which I had already witnessed, I was preparing you for the world thus I had to be persistent.

Some call it mother's intuition or say mother knows best, I am here to tell you your mother has already passed those test.
On that day when we gathered for your moment of being blessed, as God bestowed upon you a little gift knowing you are worthy of the test.
It's your contribution to the tree as our heritage grows on, so take what I've instilled in your heart and baby you can't go wrong.

Your journey has just begun and I can tell you it won't be fun, but with God on your side you'll have strength to face each rising sun.
The first test has already taken shape in that bundle of joy that you now

hold, and when thing seem to be to hard to bear just know God is in control.

So as you walk this earth and place your footprints in the sand, you are never to far from the reach of His out stretched hand.
And as your mother your friend and confidante for life, it will be the strength you find in God that will make every thing all right.

Uncharted Waters

As we get older we get wiser to the pitfalls of life, thus we tread the water lightly and hope we get it right.
For so long we've lived our lives single and unattached, and despite our relationship in the past we ponder if the next one will be a match.

We've often contemplated if ever there would be another, for truly we've rode the tide out to sea and have yet to discover.
With our faith in God and our trust in His word, we take to the sky like a free flying bird.

Looking and observing all that is around us yet never settling down, waiting on Him to deliver the one whom we will share our crown.
Sometimes the very one we seek is right before our face, that we don't realize it because we're caught between two worlds and feel it unsafe.

Even though we've witnessed the waves and know the low tides, there's something about the uncharted waters that makes us run and hide.
Not from a physical presence, but the one we value most, for truly our emotions can some times run with the waves and wash up on the coast.

Yet who among us hasn't pondered the possibilities of what might be, and some how wish they could look over the waves and see.
If by chance we get a glance of something so true and rare, one knows they are in uncharted waters but deep down they really care.

Not willing to take anything for granted as only time will reveal, truly in these uncharted waters one will see that which is concealed.
Eyes wide open as the waves are swift and moving, we pause and look to the Heaven and ask for a mental soothing.

as all kinds of thought race through our mind, we pray that the one who now stands before us is worthy of out time.
Not in the worldly sense as one has now left all that behind, knowing that one's worth is measure by that which is so heavenly divine.

$y$ou see the physical can't compare to the spiritual no matter how hard you try, and despite these being uncharted waters you've been through the fire.
Therefore let not your heart be troubled as your mind take flight, you see in these uncharted waters you have a navigator called Jesus Christ.

Chapter Six

Unspoken Words

"Words That Go Unsaid"

Black Pearls

This goes out to all my ladies of color to express how much a brother adores you and God knows there is nothing on earth I would place above you.
Truly each and every one of you are rare, from your strength and courage right down to your hair, to the sensitive side of showing a brother how much you care.

Yes, it's true some of you haven't gotten your just due, so I've composed this poem to speak on behalf of the brothers who have not a clue, there's nothing more precious than you.
Of all the jewels in the world with their colors so bright, none can compare to the black pearls for truly you are a guiding light.

With your many shades of color no earthly stone can compete, for you've withstood the test of time and never accepted defeat.
My black pearl you will forever be the rarest of stones in my eyes, as God has blessed you with a gift that keeps us alive.

Fortitude is the word that resonates through my mind, as I look back you've been the backbone and you haven't lost your shine.
What God has created on earth is a symbol of true life and beside every black man stands a black pearl as his wife.

Knowing her place as well as his, going through the rough time because to you he is all there is.
Truly the world has nothing to offer that my black pearl hasn't already found, trusting and placing your faith in Christ and living your life according to your crown.

For you are the queen of the earth forged from the rib of man, as man was brought about through sand by God's hands.
You've earned your rightful place among the highest with honors, because there are some things found within you that aren't so common.

*T*hus you stand apart from the rest, because you've simply did your best, and as I stand before the world this I must confess.
Although the other color of pearls seems to be everyone else's choice, I thank God for the rarest for it is within you my black pearl that I truly rejoice.

Her Worth

Excuse me brothers this one's for the lady who's paid her dues, and has yet to receive her accolades for what she's been through.
Those unspoken words that somehow never seemed to reach her ears, as we feel she should at least know we've been together for years.

It says a lot about us but it's not all about the man, as God created this beautiful creature for a purpose yet some fail to understand.
I was one of those for in my past I've made mistakes, blinded by ego as self-indulgence bounded my hands like the world we now see demonstrates.

Long time coming, I now feel the effect of my pain, as she is no longer with me she caught the morning train.
What she endured was by no fault of her own, it was my belief in the world that made me think I was grown.

So to her and those like her it's been a long time coming, for a man to stand before you and speak the truth without fear of him running.
Your worth can't be summed up in a few words, but what is about to be said she's never heard.
She did something that a lot of you today would never do, and I owe her my life because she helped me get through.

When all was lost and I had nothing left, she did so much more because she gave of her self.
No questions asked she just gave from the heart, as she knew what it meant to make a brand new start.
To have everything one day and then have it all taken away, she still had the courage to trust another and help him along the way.

Time got the best of me and I was unable to see, the magnitude of her worth and what it meant to me.

I would never take her for granted as she was much more, and that which I was searching for was the very thing I did ignore.
She like so many of you have moved on in life and I like so many brothers now know the ultimate price.

Although the years have gone by and so has the hurt, God has given me this time to acknowledge her worth.
They say love hurts and some say love is blind, but once you look beyond the world you see a love of a different kind.
Some don't get the chance to see and others do, and it's never to late my lady for I now see the worth in you.

The Sweetest Bouquet

As I stand over looking a garden full of flowers, I search for the one's that will reflect the trueness of your power.
Looking for the one's that will instill a sense of comfort and joy and also reflect the true sincerity of this country boy.

Knowing that you deserve the best that one can give, I must choose the flowers that display what it means to live.
They say every woman needs flowers every now and then, thus I walk through the garden to find the one that expresses a true friend.

Unlike those lost in the world I've come to understand, the true power of a flower shared between a woman and a man.
So I look to pick the ones that are a reflection of myself, and no value needs to be placed upon them because it's not according to wealth.

Therefore I look to gather those that speak from the heart, and deliver a message of love and kindness right from the start.
Also those, which confirm trust and honesty above all things, and show compassion and sincerity to which only they can bring.

Hoping they wipe away any doubt of the reason why they were given, to express deeply that life truly is worth living.
So as I stroll through the garden, I search to find the flowers, but I've yet to find the one's worthy of bringing peace like a summer rain shower.

I haven't given up hope as I look for the sweetest bouquet and there at the end of the garden I see the flowers and everything is okay.
They are not the most beautiful nor have the most vibrant colors, but they do represent the strength and determination of this brother.

You see despite their neglect and misfortunes in life, they've bloomed and became the flowers by the blessed sunlight.
Despite the day when it didn't shine, they kept growing knowing it would only be a matter of time.

Ignored by some and forgotten by most, and as I gather them together I envision you holding them so close.
You see it's not as much as the present but what they represent, as they've become the sweetest bouquet that truly is Heaven sent.

Thus I cannot take credit for the creation only the thought, and pray that they resonate through your mind and give you the peace you sought.
Each flower represents those words less spoken and taken for granted, thus no words need to be spoken as you possess the sweetest bouquet and I hope you understand it.

Tears I Cry

Truly there has to be a reason yet I often know not why, as I've yet to control my emotions and the tears I cry.
Understanding life and knowing there will be moments when I must weep, but lately it's been something I do often before I fall asleep.

As the day comes to a close I am thankful that I arose, and the tears I cry are because the world can be so cold.
My emotions are as such that I am unable to shield them from others, because God knows deep down in my heart I care for my fellow sisters and brothers.

And the tears I cry are truly not in vein, for they allow me to release my soul from the burden that has become a strain.
Knowing no matter the circumstance or the situation, as I see it, if it were not for my emotions and my passionate heart I wouldn't be able to believe it.

That the tears I cry are the very thing that makes my life worth living, because if it were not for my tears how could I express just what the Lord has given.
You see the heartache caused by the pain, which brought tears to my eyes I've come to realize that each tear I cry only, washes away and strengthens that which lives inside.

Thus I no longer hide the tears I cry, because the Lord has not forgotten me because God knows I try.
Troubling, as it may seem I know it's something that will only last for a while because in order for me to be whom I am the tears I cry only brighten my smile.

Full of life and reflect the over abundance of joy that arises from my hurt, and thus the tears I cry I now know are according to my work.
Thus I no longer hide the tears I cry, because the Lord has not forgotten me because God knows I try.

Love and Forgiveness

Love is and always has been established and sustained through forgiveness, because that love Jesus Christ had for us all then and now is endless.
That which so many of us take for granted is often revealed, yet some of us fail to see or choose not to believe.
Knowing that if love truly existed surely there would be no problems, but to fully understand the meaning of love one must be willing to solve them.

It's not easy as love can and does make one blind, thus the time we are giving one must make a conscious effort to refine.
With eyes wide open we fail to see the frailty of our human nature, not knowing that mistakes will be made according to the One who created us.
The thing with love is that we become complacent with all that it represents, that we get caught up in what the world and those in it portray as its content.

To define love one must look deep within ones self to fully understand, that love is not given yet earned by every woman and man.
Not one of us are above nor beyond the dishearten power that love can bring, because to be humble and seek or accept forgiveness is the true significant reason of that ring.
So often we look at the other and are quick to blame, that we fail to see within our selves that very thing does exist for who is without shame.

It may not be as important to you because you've become content, but surely you've done one thing that he or she may find as contempt.
You see we are assured very little in this thing we call life, and if we are to have love then we must have forgiveness to put an end to all this strife.
Love is forgiveness and forgiveness is true love, because you see without either, how can we ever hope to rise above.

Love is saying you're sorry because you simply forgot that they existed, and forgiving is acknowledging that he or she is sorry for not being persistent.

Because if one has to say they are sorry that means they forgot, and if the other is unwilling to forgive then he or she truly forgot that love takes a lot.

Jordan's River

For so long I've yearned to have my soul rest upon it's shores, and it's only a matter of time because it's something I can no longer ignore.
Battered and bruised my journey truly seems afar, but if I am to accomplish my goal I must endure theses scars.

Yes my travels have taken me near and far; this is one journey where there is no need for a car.
Although it's hard to envision I need not my sight to see, because just the thought makes my heart at ease.

Contrary to opinion it's not according to ones sight to achieve; all I need is faith and courage and the will to concede.
If you asked me am I worthy I would say no, but it is through my journey that I am allowed to grow.

I will one day walk upon the shores, as this is my testimony as I rise up from the floor.
I look upon that day as being a day of revelation, as my Lord has saw fit to deliver me unto salvation.
I look back over my life and see a person forever changing, and as I get up off my knees I realize God is forever rearranging.

Knowing on that day the world will no longer make me shiver, for each day the path brings me closer to the Jordan River.
As I draw nearer it would behoove me to give thanks, and be willing to confess all my sins before I step upon its banks.

Once there I know there's no turning back, as I step in the water I am embrace and give a joyful clap.
With raised hands I stretch out my hand unto thee, as I wade through the water my Lord becomes a bigger part of me.

*N*ot fully submerged I no longer feel the pain or the strain, before going under I take my last breathe and realize nothing else remains.
As I gather my thoughts and come up for air, the fear and anguish once felt is no longer there.

*W*ading in the middle I see the distant shore, I slowly take my time to cross over for I need nothing more.
Although cleansed by the water I am purified by His blood, thus I know the true meaning of unconditional love.

*R*eaching the shore I know there's no need to look back, for I've left nothing behind as my Lord Jesus Christ has assured me of that.
You see despite it all I've kept the faith for I knew He would deliver, thus I am at peace for my soul salvation shall come once I cross the Jordan River.

My Gift to You

As I ponder the thought of what I wish to give to you, I know in my heart that it has to be something true.
What can it be, because I know there is something you need, so I take a moment and step away from the world before I proceed?

I take this time to reflect upon the times we've shared, and I realize it must be something to show you how much I really care.
No diamonds or pearls can express the way I truly feel, thus my search continues as I search for that which is real.

Neither fur nor mink coat could show my appreciation for you, thus I won't give up until my journey is through.
Although frustrated and confused I reach deep within to find strength, and at that moment the Lord shared with me that gift, and what it meant.

I dare not question that which had been revealed; knowing that the truest gift one can give is being for real.
I looked for a box to place it in yet there was none big enough, I tried wrapping paper and a ribbon but that I did not trust.

What could it be that nothing could hold or would suffice well it's a gift that keeps on giving and it's a thing called life.
Filled with friendship and trust, honesty and respect with unconditional love, you see that which I'd been searching for is what we share simply because.

There's much more to life than the material things, for we have been blessed with a friendship, oh what joy it brings.
Unwavering and undaunted, forthright and inspiring, truly its priceless there is no denying, thus I vow to keep on trying.

Although words are often spoken at times they fall on deaf ears, so I gathered them all together as a gift to my closest friend whom I hold so dear.

Chapter Seven

With You in Mind

"Words to soothe a troubled spirit"

A Better Understanding

*A*lthough we may lose a loved one in our life, we never lose the life of that loved one day or night.
There are so many memories for one to cherish, beyond the realm their own existence once they perish.
Knowing one has grown accustomed and appreciated them while they where living, the love and emotional ties formed will never stop giving.
For truly the love that was shared will never die, thus the love that one has shall always remain alive.

*H*ard to comprehend the lost of someone so dear, but take comfort in knowing that Jesus Christ holds them near.
Thus a better understanding shall come of what has taken place, and joy will replace the tears that run down your face.
Realizing that their life has come full circle according to His grace and their pain is washed away without a trace.
The writing was on the wall as they found peace from within, and a better understanding of the Holy Comforter who was their closest friend.

*S*eeing a love so great come to the end of their reign on earth, one should be glad that they had an opportunity to share in their wealth.
Realizing that in death there is a rebirth of one's soul, and although they are gone they left you with so much because of what was told.
Truly that is something, which will remain stored away deep in your heart, as you find comfort in knowing they made a new start.
So as you pray for a better understand of life as it comes to an end, realize the Farther will provide the answer and give you peace from within.

*G*rasping the realness that it was only the flesh that was lost, and that He is in full control of the soul we loved who paid the cost.
He will bless you with a better understanding and give you comfort in time, because the spirit of the one you loved is taken to a higher level and is doing fine.
Giving you the strength to stand as a pillar among the many, and allow

you to provide others with a better understanding when they can't find any.

Knowing that all is not lost through death yet one must appreciate the gain, and recognize the beauty of it all and pray that you'll be able to see them once again.

Holding On

Living in a world of uncertainty and facing the unknown, we know our day will come if we just hold on.
As each day changes like the weather, we know in our hearts that things will get better.
Yet our mind takes over and we wonder what to do, as we sit saying to ourselves, "I've got to make it through."

Feeling like the weight of the world rests upon your shoulders, is there any one out there to help, as we get older?
Doing your best to take care of the rest, you know you will be blessed if only you make it through this test.

Yes, the heart feels heavy and the body needs a break, but you can't walk away from the decision you did make.
Knowing there are others who are not fairing so well, you often reminisce of the stories they tell.

Holding on to something that really needs to be let go, they cling to it ever so tightly letting their feelings show.
Knowing the answers to their questions they can't face the facts, feeling they've come too far and there's no turning back.

Knowing in their heart that someone or some thing no longer exists, they keep holding on trying to create that which they miss.
Until one day the burden becomes too great and the pain too intense, they realize holding on is not the good Lords intent.

Holding on to the memory of what was but not to forget, that tomorrow brings anew and let go of all the regret.
You can't change the world only you that live within it, thus hold on to what's really important and stay committed.

Not what was but what surely is to be, so what if you can't see, all you have to do is believe.
In yourself is truly the first step, and not look to any other for help, because Jesus Christ heard your cries as you wept.

You see in letting go you allow Him the use of your hands, and He'll place within them a promise worth holding on and this you will come to understand.

Sunrise

The dawning of a new day, I am thankful to be alive, in a world where so much is taken for granted -- I value this sunrise.
As I have yet to become complacent and not notice what's before my eyes, as each morning I awake brings a new day and it's up to me to try.

Not to conquer the world but simply to understand it much better, for each day brings us a message we just have to figure out each letter.
Thus I can not let that which I feel is personal take over my life, because I've been granted another day to get things right.

As each transformation take place way up in the sky, there is a bigger one going on with me deep down inside.
Although the colors may not show for the whole world to see, I am grateful for the sunrise knowing it is because of me.

As there is no greater divide than Heaven and Earth, but by His grace each sunrise bridges that divide thus symbolizes its worth.
Thus each morning I arise with a smile as the sun shines in my eyes and I look forward to the many gifts and each wonderful surprise.

For truly I am blessed and can not start my day unless I confess, that although I am not worthy give me strength and courage to face each test.
Because at that moment in time I was allowed to marvel God's work, thus as I go about my day because that which follows is according to my worth.

As the sunrise breaks through the clouds despite their persistence, it transcends down upon us and brings to light the meaning of our existence.
You see this day is truly like no other, as it's not taken for granted for each step allows me to travel that much further.
Not to a certain place or by a certain time, as it to a place in His time that truly no words can define.

The Burden

*O*f our existence bears no weight that we should not be willing to carry, for in these troubled times let not one of us tarry.
Yet despite our best efforts we often carry more than was meant to be, and forever struggle to do such an easy thing as opening our eyes to see.
Why we are unable to is because of our own admission, and the burden gets heavier for we aren't willing to submission.

*T*he weight of the world is not on your shoulders; you just never prepared yourself for when you got older.
We expect so much out of life that it passes us by, and that's why when we are faced with the burdens of life we often cry.
Not knowing the full extent of that which we carry, we often retreat behind a wall for surely it's scary.
Ironic enough it's the little thing that bears the most weight, and no matter how big the wall we can't see straight.

*W*hy is that maybe we constructed the wall from the outside in, not knowing if we did it from the inside out we'd find a friend?
You know that friend in time of trouble, willing to share the load and most of all willing to walk with you down the middle of the road.
Yes such a person does exist, for as many times as you've wished; Jesus Christ was there if only you unclenched your fist.
You see 99.9 % of the burden we carry is not meant for us, He's only asking for 10 % -- we are the ones who make it tuff.

*N*ot willing to see things for what they are, we have to make them bigger than life and wonder why we have the scars.
Battered and bruised and we've yet to see the light, carrying more than we ought to for fear of giving of the fight.
Just understand neither the battle nor the burden is yours to carry what is, is submission and omission is so let us not tarry.

Knowing the Truth

Truly is the one thing in life that often eludes us, but no matter how hard we try it's something that at some point excludes us.
It's like you do your very best to be honest and forthright, not taking anything for granted for all that you have is in plain sight.
Yet we ourselves fail to see things the way they really are, because despite another telling the truth you remember the scars.

You see knowing the truth is one thing, but living it and accepting is hard because of what it means.
We seek that which is true and honest everyday at least that's what we hope, then and thing called reality hits you and you find it was just a joke.
It's all about what one perceives yet fails to realize they have yet to receive, and to face not knowing the truth make it even harder for one to believe.
Where does it start or how does one know that which is to be true, it's very simple because truth must first start within you.

If you know that which to be true then no other person can confuse you and make you have doubt if you know the clues.
Therefore any one or anything which come before you truly has it place, and just because you can't see it doesn't mean it doesn't exist within their face.
Knowing and accepting the truth about self is the first step, and despite what may not be the truth you'll always maintain your self-respect.
There is not one among us that would rather be told we just need to understand the truth and not lose control.

So, many of us let our thoughts and what we think it should be, cloud our judgment not knowing it only makes it that much harder to see.
Be willing to accept it for what it is and take a step back, and look within ones self and review all the facts.
The truth is as the truth does, and if truth is within you then you simply must rise above.

Love's Journey

We go through life seeking a treasure more precious than gold, for truly it is priceless with wealth untold.
Knowing God has blessed you with a gift that can't be put into words, as no writer or poet could express that feeling that already hasn't been heard.
It come from within the soul and that a sacred domain, and to find true love you know your life will never be the same.

Its journey can take you places you've never been before; it can also make you blind to what it may have in store.
It can start along a two way street but you end up on a one-way road, or it can put you on easy street because there is someone to share the load.
Showing you along the way it's the little things that mean so much, as they will bring you through the hard times when things get ruff.

Yet some take it for granted or are just along for the ride, not knowing that once you're on this journey one must swallow their pride.
There is a price to pay as it can surely takes its toll, but for each one that you pass through there will be one waiting to console.
That's the true beauty of this journey, which will never change, as long as you are willing to give your all in order to maintain.

Yes, it's easy to get off track and lose you way, but just remember love is more than just the words you say.
It's an endless journey with no destination in mind, so look not beyond the one before you because no other shall you find.
Thus you share a ring with another as you take your ride, and vow that no other shall destroy that which comes from inside.

So, if by chance the road seems unclear and you're unable to see your way, look inside your self and take a moment to pray.
Not for direction but for the imperfection and stay where you are and

let Christ meet you in the intersection.
And He'll show you the sign and no longer will you hope wishfully, because the sign He holds reads love unconditionally.
Because the love journey you've taken is a never-ending voyage, and as long as you travel with Him in mind you'll never run out of storage.

That Which I Owe

With all the wealth and fame that shower so many, I am of a humble beginning saving every penny.
I may not have much but my wealth goes way beyond theirs, because no amount of money can change the way I care.

Although my debt may seem to be overwhelming I am a wealthy man, you see that which I owe is truly out of my hands.
It reaches way beyond their thinking or them being able to understand, that no amount of money can pay that which God holds in His hands.

Living within the realm of what my life has come to be, I dare not stray from that path despite all the things I see.
The finer things in life have given away to living a refined life, and that which I owe is truly worth the price.

Once I was consumed by the world and was paying a price, for something I would never own, it just seemed right.
Never fully understanding the logic like so many of us today, I placed a value on the material not knowing it would soon fade away.

Like so many if I could name it then I would claim it, then one day I felt the shame in it and knew I had to refrain from it.
Coming of age one must be willing to turn the page and that which you owe is a payment that must be made.

Not to the bill collector, nor to the bank, because that which you owe is truly your way of saying thanks.
Not for what you have, but for that which you've been given, a right and a promise through Christ that allows you to keep on living.

So you see that which I owe, is what allows me to grow, it's not what I know but who I know, and I am willing to pay the price for that which I owe.

Author's Biography

MARCELLUS T. DEAN

I was born and raised in Aldie, Virginia a small rural town outside of Washington D.C. where everyone in the neighborhood knew each other. Throughout my childhood and teenage years, I like so many others was brought up in the church. I grew up learning the teachings of the gospel as my mother instilled it in me. I found wisdom an understanding of life and what it has to offer, through the elders of our quaint little town. I learned that "Respect" is truly the one thing, which helped me through my many years in the U.S. Army. Trusting and believing in God has sustained me throughout my life, knowing that through Him all things are possible. The last ten years I've experienced many of life's trials and tribulations but through His love and mercy, I've become the pen that writes messages of hope and understanding. This gift that I've received from God has allowed me as well as others to find healing from within, thus my mission in life is to share that which was given unto me with the world. Through reflection one will be blessed with a revelation and find peace from within and understand one's self better. This book is lovingly dedicated to my grandmother, Emma Bell Smith, although gone her love lingers on and I thank God for her.

Printed in the United States
113652LV00002B/1-99/P